MOVING

TO

COMPLETION

MOVING

TO

COMPLETION

John Fitzpatrick

FOR

Cecelia Schmidt Fitzpatrick
my courageous and loving mother

Dorcas Watters
an encouraging and supportive poet-friend

Lynn Hoins
a trusted poet-friend, adviser, and supporter

Gary Clark
a wonderful encourager and visionary adviser, poet-friend

Rob Stolzer
an adventurous artist who gifted his intriguing art work

Shelley Meisler
a talented poet, writer. jeweler, painter, who helps me succeed

Todd Vogel
a splendid photographer, writer, novelist, electronic genius,
offering his talent for my success

**Jeanne Cameron—John Cardano—Susan Kern
Simone Butler**
as intuitive spirit-guides for helping me advance
in earthly and spiritual realms

and

All Animal-Spirits
who have communicated with me along the way

Order this book: www.magcloud.com

Copyright © 2012 John Fitzpatrick

All rights reserved.

No part of this book may be reproduced, stored in a retrieval system or transmitted by any means, electronic, digital, mechanical, photocopy, recording, or by any other means, without prior written permission of the author, except for brief quotations embodied in critical articles and reviews.

Printed in the United States on acid-free paper

ISBN: 978-0-9883403-0-5

Publisher: turtleamipress
PO Box 644
Rhinebeck NY12572-0644

Editor: Lynn Hoins

Photography: Todd Vogel, ODATBooks.com

Painting: Shelley Meisler

Art Work: Rob Stolzer, www.robstolzer.com

Author Photograph: Howard Romero,
    Vermont Studio Center

TABLE OF CONTENTS

begin with tone	1
I Am Turtle	2
Motion	4
Waters Turned Into Harp	6
Dragonfly,	9
Night Granary Rest	10
The Moth	12
Squirrel Self	15
Nature's Intrigue	17
Remembering	18
A Bird's Lament	21
Fair Warning	23
Visitor	26
Sojourner	27
The Calling	30
Gathering	32
Night Visitors	33
Beach Walk	36
Flesh Bait	37
Mating Season	38
I Needed Support This Week	40
Over Shimmering Water	41
Unaltered	43
Return From Windham	44
The Prickly Ones	46
On Meeting An Ant	48
Tomorrow	51
Spider	52
Sparrow	54
Traveling The Edge	55

begin with tone

I saw infinity through mist this morning
enticing me to come inside, imagine

what was beyond. I heard life grow
by listening to the Gihon rippling over rocks

on which algae glisten. Sounds of language
have come within words used, rhythms spoken,

read, written, painted. Calmness came
inside me when I was willing to flow

through any situation. I was liquidity
standing still. Serenity in motion,

a ruby throated hummingbird moving
yet not moving; this bumblebee traveling

bloom to bloom, content and self-assured.
I have climbed mountains standing

in place and through my eyes,
traversed those distances with ease.

I Am Turtle

I explore earth's regions, dark
edges of forests, even marsh lands,
swim watery depths, gaining
experience all the time. On land,

I bask in the sun and sleep
in warm folds of self, where I
withdraw inward, there to dream
visions of an ancestor spirit. I link

earth to water, water to earth,
a cycle of eternal balance. I carry
my world with me. My shell and I
are one, house and home I never

leave. I lay my future on shore
and hope my generations survive.
Should water submerge these places,
I will exist no more, only as art,

primeval image of what once was.
Perhaps return in another form.
When I am flipped, I claw the air.
Reach back with neck. Push head

against ground. With roll, regain balance
through strength, perseverance. I am
alone from start. Drawn to water as soon
as I leave birth sands of darkness.

I am secure in myself. My lumbering pace
belies my nature, full of ageless wonder.
My artwork I carry with me, upper and
lower realms, cycles of twelve carved

in designs of mystery. My obstacles are
many. I go around them. I look forward.
Live in the moment. Have no attachments.
I am turtle. Ancient and forever.

-for Glennis Drew

Motion

Honestly, tadpoles grow into frogs.
    Or do frogs emerge
        from length of movement?

The swirl, the swag,
    the back and forth
        of water churning desire into form.

There is no other way to explain it —
    this essence of one's self
        moving to completion.

Waters Turned Into Harp

> "He gathers the waters of the seas
> as a harp." Psalm 32

Fish help out. Dolphins, too.
    They churn waters for weaving,
        the bringing together. As if distaff

and spindle collecting, spinning,
    crossing lengths into one strand,
        certainly more, beyond number.

Emotions that vibrate energy,
    in darkness, in light. Colors,
        the spectrum of wonder,

that chakras claim each for own.
    Red for earth. Orange for water
        cleansing, bringing life

from earthen mother lode. Yellow
    for *dan tian*. Beyond these,
        green, blue, violet, white,

full spectrum from which, within which,
    others twirl and create. Stand alone.
        Dissolve. Like reflections from

deep deep sea. Its waves find harmony,
        resolve discord. Turn into tendrils
                of music plucked and strummed.

Each vibration, a player, a listener, the same.
        Whales bring depth and mystery.
                Breaching surface for air and light.

Dolphins join in. Other fish, too.
        They break into sunshine.
                Those even in depth, providing

undertone. Their modulation,
        water quivering in sunlight.
                In moon time, too. Beauty,

this gathering of waters into harp of song.

Dragonfly,

with your red linked tail, long,
and your body fur lined on top

and your double tufts of russet
on double gossamer wings,

guided by boulder black eyes,
you keep returning to my pant leg,

a very bleak flower. You nibble
but nothing is there — no thread loose,

no sweetness, no pollen to carry away —
yet you come back resting on this drab earth

lolling in the sun — wings wavering as if to shake
out air! Will you last another year? Will you

be here when I return hence, if ever?
You do not know nor I — nor should you—

this lazy autumn day lounging on my chino leg —
drawing what you can from the rest you seek

and from the color you may never know again.
O crimson bird of flight ride with me

as long as you like. Then rest beyond
your resting and fly beyond your flight.

-for Maryalice Johnston and Michael Burkard

Night Granary Rest

Burnt red tower dark dawn perch
of birds in row of prayer
meditating for oncoming day

as I ponder travel looking inward
for destiny's calling. Rocks haphazard
in River of Gihon surface rushing torrent of water

admiring earth's blooming that begins
with lines of cabs stuck in traffic,
themselves bubble shaped, yellow,

lights gone out from evening trolls.
Stillness inside depending on customer
who asks for places to go into darkness,

sex driven or culture driven, perhaps
alcohol driven, that has churned coherency
into raging river before me, bubbling along the way,

driven as by desire for answers that never come
at end of meandering search until cashier
asks for payment, after the act, usually before,

then wing stretches, first the right,
left next, scaly legs lift from bed
of roof as I exercise to limber up body

prone from evening rest, and I rise off edge
gathering momentum for flight
to end dull journey of searching for purpose,

no answers, only rock surfacing impediments
I speed around in yellow flight to sit here
on tall granary marooned for the night

until daybreak comes, and I lift head from wing
in morning fling with river of air.

The Moth

You held there close to a week,
sucked whiteness from the curtain.
Your dark stained wings moved not

nor bleached light from this food.
You only waited, waited through the glare
of days and evenings, while each one passed,

came and went as to some master
in contemplation. Here you came,
after long journey through fields

for an ecstasy of dance. Now tired, you cling
to silence, move only as shadow to the sun
and the night air toward this draw of light.

At first, I thought of sending you
to the nether world. But you were there already,
on the wall of this primordial cave. And I felt

an affinity for you. Your marks intrigued me.
Dark stripes that winged back into gentleness.
Underneath, a nap of lighter tan, a winter coat

worn in torrid August. Brown quilted fur.
Black dots as eyes that mushroomed
from the earth. Now, you starve,

thin yourself into a sacred wafer,
stuck on this cave's palate, roof-tight.
It is an effort to get you off,

to swallow your meaning.
You put yourself there, drew yourself
from the brush of the shaman,

from the very depth of his spirit
where you lived in the dark crimson
that flowed through his body.

He toiled with twigs and filaments of animal hair,
the dyes of herbs and berries on cool dirt
smoothed by rough stubble of fingers.

Each day he came to bless your progress,
to work magic with his elements.
The flicker of oil turning darkness into bones,

flesh where there was no flesh.
Shade where fullness was needed.
The journey, not easy, the recesses of longing

gathering strength for the long passage.
You came as if the force of nature had willed it.
First, the urge — that quiet ache

that consumes the nerves.
Then the push, the force of becoming.
Each limb, each part of you, ached itself

into existence, into the folds of consciousness,
where you tumbled through the orifice of light,
window of this cave. Each time I returned,

you were there, one with this cavern wall.
Lone figure in hoarfrost. The press of your
presence, a fossil now in my memory.

I paid you homage.
You took my breath
to vault into the blue gentian sky.

-for Kathy Fogarty

Squirrel Self

I

I killed a squirrel this morning.
It dashed out before me on I-90,

hesitated then sped back as if needing
to return for some forgotten item.

Oh, I saw him way ahead of me.
His speed to get across the road.

His stop. His pause. His turn.
I admired the ease with which

he accomplished this feat like
some athlete in morning exercise.

But lost in ecstasy of his swiftness,
I swerved the wrong way.

II

Days earlier beside the Roe Jan Kill,
I placed on a branch all my doubts

and weaknesses and flung it
into cascading waters then looked

upstream in prayer for openness of heart.
I left this river full of commitment

to follow my new path. Next morning
my anxieties returned along with aches and pain

of body still weak from disease and stress
and overactive herbs. I hesitated. Turned.

Fought panic for air and resuscitation.
Later that day, I thought, *Get up,*

recommit, breathe Spirit air. Now,
out of reverie, I am back on I-90.

I look in rear view mirror. See squirrel,
its feet in air, squashed again by another car.

I speed on, wondering if I have enough time
to make it across my own imaginary highway.

Nature's Intrigue

lichen hugs contours of rock
barnacles surface with breaching whale
nature's embrace, the need of security

leaf hesitates leaving branch
wren ponders build on top of sill or under canopy
safety's anguish, the dilemma of tomorrow

gossamer entices victim
Venus flytrap lures unsuspecting
desire's entrapment, the rhythm of survival

rattler injects venom
hornet stuns provocateur
foe's vanquish, the art of surprise

flower nectar attracts honeybees
mating season trills into dance
earth's instincts, the ecstasy of fulfillment

Remembering

I

It must be esoteric.
Magical in imagery.
Convoluted in form.
Obscure, even ambiguous

in its dexterity to solve
any problem
yet not solve it
for what is the benefit

if the sum total of existence
matches not the inner state
of my essence? Dinner
is late. I forgot some

ingredients so I had
to go out. No I didn't.
Just pick up phone and order.
Delivery came in form

of a circle, distorted
by rush of placing halves
in a box created to solve
a problem. Magical I thought.

Even down right obscure
in its practicality to grant
ambiguity an existence
it wanted but could not have.

II

I am told I must go deep
into my inner self. Look back
into the obscurity of infancy.
Then along the way

break up all blockages,
rather declare all traumas
of my being. Hang it all
up there blimp-like

over a stadium of a thousand,
rather thousands,
ten thousand, twenty perhaps,
forty maybe, depending on where

the fetal position is,
what part of my
existence is where
in this tunnel I am

descending. A labyrinth.
The bad part . . .
as I descend I forget
to let out the string.

I no spider that dangles
from ceiling of my present
to chasm below. How
am I to get back once

I proclaim my catharsis
in this echo chamber? I'm stuck here
having gone only twenty-three leagues
below the surface of my memory.

I wish I had paid more attention
to how the spider does it.

A Bird's Lament

Even when I struggle to grip
this branch, these clawed feet
lose their way to hold onto ideas.
It is all in the feet — the balance of the world.
I used to think it was in my head, this holding on.
But it has come to this — holding on with the feet.
Nodding off with head under wing
hoping these claws stay.

My strength dissipates
like veins in a leaf
trailing off into the wide
space of nothing. A long distance
there. Time when I must listen.
The measurement of self into space
beyond which there is only sky,
heights I can not scale. My wings too weak.

I cough a lot now.
My head dizzy.
I had wanted to chase
this monster that bothered me at feeding time.
This sleek black drone that shadowed his presence
even before he came. His cool darkness sent

shivers through me. Sun blotted out.
Thoughts of ebony. This cowering
in the face of finality.

Each day limitations come.
Land blurs when I look down.
Lines that were there
cross one another as dark spaces.
Just when I marvel at the scene below,
breath gives way, and I glide
into dreams. Even now,
I know it has come to this —

the holding on. My bones send me
to deep quiet of self.
I listen. Glance at my feet.

Fair Warning

Late at night. A mirage. Or just a creature
        lumbering over my papers as I bend down
                to retrieve some lost idea I thought

might be in transit through mail without
        proper postage, with no ZIP code at all,
                not even a phone number to call

its sender to ask, *Did you perhaps see*
        what I just saw crawling from this crevice
                that joins your house with mine,

thousand of miles away, a fault line
        over which a nuclear plant is built,
                the kind found in California,

even maybe elsewhere, the type found
        to be safe by the NRC regardless
                of geological split, not the atom,

merely a divide that keeps separating and
        separating over time the way creatures do
                and humans do and all living things

do at the end when we break apart
        and away which is exactly
                what happened here from the time

I saw this prehistoric creature late at night
  in my studio to the time I came early
    to write this morning, like the time

I found it in my Lascaux cave,
  or the time I painted it on temple walls,
    even the time I chiseled it in stone,

sculptured it with my hands in clay,
  wrought it in iron as a pin for my friend
    who wanted a copy, not the real

animal crawling around at home,
  curse of homeowners who hate
    its distractions day and night,

and again next morning, endless noise?
  But here it is now, work time,
    this long dark creature

with elevated legs, two in front,
  another two but smaller close by,
    and two that spring back with long

extensions that bend down to ground.
  A plumber's delight. This use of pipe.
    This artisan smithy design

painted black. Are they always black?
  My uncle would tell me as a child,
    Be not afraid of it. Listen

for its sound. When you hear it,
    know it will be six weeks
        *to winte*r. Or was it eight?

I forget. But I remember
    the essence of what he had to say.
        This harbinger gives a warning.

Prepare. Get the crops in.
    The writing done. The car ready
        so when fissure splits, we move

fast. Even faster than nuclear meltdown.
    Faster than the reaper who shows up
        when least expected and flips us

on our backs, no more to rise. Apparently
    last night, this cricket sounded the alarm.
        Then did its acrobatic flip to time.

-for Glennis Drew

Visitor

Taken by itself,
the red plump tomato

hangs precariously
in empty belly moon light

until it releases its form
to claws that seek it.

Sojourner

I spend hours,
days, trying
to control pests,
insects,
rid them from my porch,
my house, the yard,
cracks, the night air,

even resolve
to spray, set traps,
until culprits lay
vanquished,
dead or near death.
Now, here

one comes,
surfaces through
the crevice of these
porch boards,
a bug never

seen before,
never prepared for,
a sleek red shelled body,
its parts, tuned,
layer, upon layer,

moving.
I stand over it,
now kneel,
to look closer

at thin neck,
thinner tail,
body moved by hundreds,

perhaps thousands
of minuscule legs
in front end leaps as if
to see down some canyon trail
test some height,
some invisible wall
to climb, preach
from, precursor
of some far-off world

that calls to me,
my thought forming
a story of worlds
I run from,
spray from,
invisible dark
worlds of memory
recalled. *Danger*.

Are you dangerous?

Two head antennas,
pincer tail,
always moving,
slashing a path

I want
to follow,
my mind's eye, hand

ready for combat,
intrigued,
dangerous, ready for
journey into the unknown.
Attack.

I take you
in, draw you
on the folds of my mind,
where you speak
to me, lead
me through dungeons

tonight,
in my dreams
where I serve you,
red oared creature.
Live.

-for Michael Burkard

The Calling

A great migration continued
above gray overcast of day.
The sound, honks of reminders
to get tasks done, tent mended,
wood gathered, dung collected
and peat cut for the long winter fires.
It is the season where each finds a place to die.
The calling, voices from the sky
that say: *Make peace with yourself,
let go of living, come here with us,
to the higher region, as your ancestors did.*

Each time the call came, they left,
followed the sound to a place no one knows.
Alone, they went to wait the time
when the voice would say, *Come with me,*
and there in the woods, on a high cliff,
in some cave, they would step out of themselves
to go the long distance from where no one returns.

Today, all day, sounds have come.
They have said to me: *Prepare yourself.*
Take the high precipice above the canoe crossing
and leap into sky with us.
At that moment, you will grow wings.
They will mend strong with journey
and be healed in the time it will take to join us.
The sound of leaving will be wind
coming to lift you here with us.
You go where feathers will be grown
and you will be like us, the ancients.

I prepare to go,
to join my sisters and brothers overhead.
Already wings come
and my webbed feet lift off into sky.

Gathering

The silent darkness of the cricket people
settled in the corner of bad luck
where early predictions were told.
The candle light grew more intently,
where the glow of silver tresses
hung beyond shoulders.
One evening, these same children
crept from their hiding places,
past the cauldron of séances
into the opening of trees.
It was not yet time
for stars to signal
their messages. Too late
for morning delivery.
Winter was seven weeks away.

Night Visitors

I spied them first
        across
the summer evening,
        spinning up clouds
of reddish shadow,
        all shifting downward
skimming the horizon

        in a staggering display
of virtuosity
        welcoming tomorrow —
a wondrous whirling,
        dipping, surfacing —
one gliding
        to stop

on crystal clear edge
        of water fountain,
clamping tight;
        another on branch
swinging, bobbing, clinching,
        its edge of tail feathers
a redant brown,

             springing up and down;
wings close
          to cylinder breast,
brighter red,
          soft brighter red,
brownish in hue,
          lighter throat

pulsing note in,
          note out,
its head
          darker crowned
curved downward
          to twitching tail,
at rest, observant,

          holding
for whatever water
          is left.
Morning has come;
          my partner gone, early.
The sky aqua
          and vibrant,

Monet almost,
          and the branches
filled with moving
          avians, pausing,
swirling in and out,
          down and back,
necks gulping

                slide of water taken.
One alights
                on clothesline,
joins flap
                of shirts swaying
in gentle breeze.
                Tail flipping

in syncopation
                with Colors Benetton.
This mix
                of creation
excites
                my desire to rise
beyond self.

                Its reddish
brown breast
                heaving chirps
to rippled sky
                waiting turn
to drink
                the water air.

-after Robert Dana

Beach Walk

When my father went away,
he did not tell me he would draw
the water about him,

curl himself into the shell of a mollusk,
and turn his skin into alabaster.

He did not see me come to him
that winter morning he lay on the ocean shore,
his mouth to the sky,
his curved back bedded in debris.

Nor was he there
when I picked him up.

Flesh Bait

Wading in Bradner Creek,
I make friends with minnows.
They nibble at my feet, mainly tips

of toes. Some try to swim
under my arches. Most prefer
to stay away from those tunnels,

going for more open spaces
in case this flesh bait takes them away.
Inquisitive, these fish.

Because they are young, untested?
How big can they get
in this creek that gets no deeper

than below my ankles?
Where do they go when
their weight and size tell them

this stream is no place to be,
except perhaps to spawn?
Below this stream, there is

deeper pond, some nine feet
and more, our favorite swimming hole.
There, they nibble less at our bodies,

giant whales plunging in and out.
They go deeper and deeper
to explore the caverns of survival.

Mating Season

-To the young child who exclaimed upon looking
up at the twin towers, "Look, teacher, the birds
are on fire."
        The New York Times, September 18, 2001

The towers fell inward
like an onion that wraps itself
layer upon layer, tight,
to protect itself, to protect
its inner core, like a human
who searches inward to come
to pure essence of self,
to pure essence of life.
The birds, too, when they
close their eyes searching
darkness they see before them.
What plumage to put on
for the mating season — the male
resplendent in its garb to attract
desired female or the female
resplendent in its garb to attract
desired male who will
give her offspring,
the best of offspring.
Here, perched high,
story upon story,
persons don robes
turned into fire
as old as Medea's

revenge on Jason,
to plunge
into morning sky
already rolling with ash
to become birds
of flight, gliding, circling,
abandoning self
in a mating dance
to air, in an ashen glide
that catches the eyes of a child
who looks upward
at this strange dance
and chooses
with words and image
to mate with history
destined to produce
offspring of pure
remembrance.

I Needed Support This Week

-Inspired by John Cardano and Kerry Hardie

I read his book again about pain into health.
I also read her poem about a girl visiting
a sheep auction. I imagine there is shit all around.
I observe how a woman breast feeds her baby
while the auctioneer continues to sell sheep,
mindless of anything else.

My shit is inside me. I trudge through it every day.
The auctioneer is me, trying to sell me
whatever formula looks best for my condition.
I bid on everything. Can't make up my mind.
I take home what I buy, try it out, become what I
try. Only I'm dissatisfied. What I bought doesn't

feed me. Doesn't give enough milk so I can grow.
I return. Bid on another approach. The shit
continues. Every day. Every moment. I haven't
found an animal I like best. Not even me. So, I bid
again, never realizing I control the bidding.
I control the amount of shit I have accumulated.

I control the breast milk I feed on, bid on, bring
home to grow on. This sheep is me. This buyer,
too. If I would shut up, stop the bidding, halt my
buying, I think the shit would stop and I would
treat myself as a person should be treated,
with dignity, no matter my gender or my needs.

Over Shimmering Water

a great blue heron

wings the shoreline seeking guests

to invite for dinner

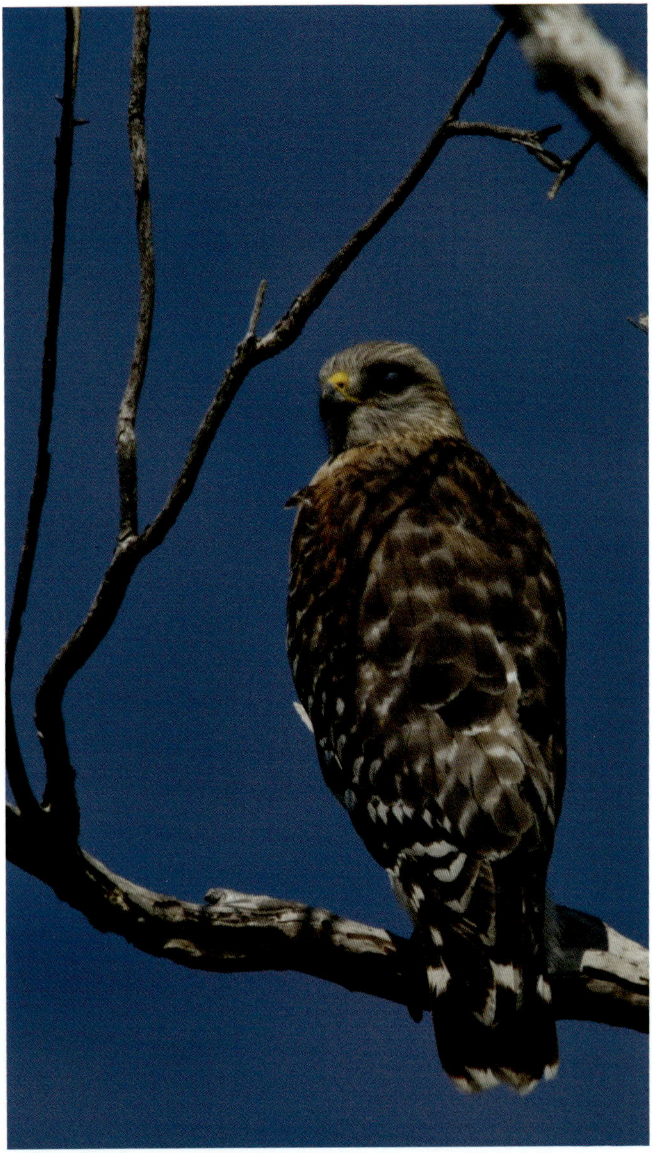

Unaltered

A red-tailed hawk sits on limb
scanning field for movement.

A reclusive green heron stands
in river stream eyeing its next prey.

Crows scavenge roadway
for carcass, their delicacy of choice.

Above, under descending gray,
legions of geese prepare to mirror

themselves in lake of images.
There, on pine bough,

spindly hands hold cone
nibbling want into fullness.

I have not put out food
this season. It is my desire

to avoid consequences.
Now, earth fends for itself.

The way it always has.

Return From Windham

Death has ridden with me
this long drive home, caught in space
between headlight and bumper rim,
wings arched still as if free in flight,
its warm body wrapped in soft blue-gray feathers.

I in my armor wish for sail of air,
roll of wind that would lift me
to such promontory vision.
It is too much to ask forgiveness,
too much to intone the Requiem.

There, under this dark circumference,
you rest, a sacrifice on this altar of Hephaestus.
Faraway, there is a special plot of land
for my deceased childhood friends:
the rabbit taken too soon from its mother,

the pink squeal of mice found after the mower
had gone, others who curled themselves around
woolen time. All buried in hollows dug
with young hands, the earth more fertile
with these offerings. Deep grass soon to ebb close

my memory until the next grief.
This cemetery grew near a black gnarled
cherry tree whose gum pitched bark glistened
mirror-like in daytime. In season its fruit became
the feast of starlings. Their droppings, ground

offerings for those who rested below. They
would screech their Sanctus as I placed parts
of myself into a cardboard box to be set adrift
in seagrass. That place is too distant now
for you to join these relics of my youth.

Here, I will measure out a new field
in this adulthood of my longing.
Under this oak sapling I will bury you
to grow strong and tall, to shadow
the land with your wing-éd flight.

The Prickly Ones

They stood open in the rolling fields,
bunched together here and there,
as few plants would dare grow near them
or be snagged in their barbed leaves
which really weren't leaves
but protruding stalks,
short,
stem-like.

With them came neatly packed flowers,
purple, a lighter tint within
their circular crown of fluff,
drawn tightly inside their bristly pods.

Only butterflies of the rarest kind
came to light on their soft cushions.
They would ease down,
carefully,
as if they feared
a stab
or a needle prick,
or just hover by,
close enough to sip
the pollen
and the nectar scent.

Strange . . .
only the solitary ones
came
and then fluttered
on
satisfied
that all was not
that bad with thistles.

-for John J. and Katherine
          Gregorius Schmidt & Family

On Meeting An Ant

I work down
from top shelves
to the lowest
soon to floor itself

where with wet sponge
I crawl my destiny

like others I meet along the way.
One stops,
its black ovals wired fast,
the last of a long line

stretched out like pack horses
down canyon trails.

At first we only stare
then move closer where we scan
for sameness, examine appendages,
like medics.

Sounds are floated.
Garbled, they are hard to understand.

Then childlike
I jabber echoes in return.
They soon match,
break open upon one another.

We begin to talk,
to reveal ourselves.

We tell each other our burdens:
the endless task of movement,
the up and down of summer.
Of objects that fall from the sky

and spring into air again —
they move us off course

and crush dreams underneath.
Streams we drink from burn.
The forage we live on fevers.
Now, others continue by.

Pause, they join us.
One is my neighbor.

We recognize each other.
They ask us along
to visit awhile,
to share the weight of distance.

A huge crumb is placed in my mouth.
Another is lifted on my back.

My pockets are filled bulging.
They begin to move
across cleaned tile. And I,
I fall in line.

Tomorrow

My uncle, near ninety,
talks about death
as if it were tomorrow.
Today he gives himself
to explore his garden.

There, wooden stakes bend under their load.
Plump red giants play mountain-king
with each snap of his wrist.
Distant mounds ripple
as gourds turn for comfort,
circle the ground like dogs for the right form.
Treasures are dug aged in darkness.

His life comes to him
like vapors that rise each evening,
guests out of the darkness
uninvited but in the area.

I do not think he minds the wait.
He could go now if he felt that way.
I temper his talk —
tell him to plan for distant years.
He sets aside all excuses.

I go to sleep certain of no nightly visitors.
He listens to the wind.

-for my uncle, Frank J. Schmidt

Spider

I see you wrap your prey in comfort,
send it into deep sleep, assured
it will feel no draft so tight your love

for this gift from Great Spider Spirit.
You build more dream catchers.
Soon, bring forth own kind. Children

independent from birth, with no mothering,
no feeding, no marsupial love. You
whisper to me, *I am Birth Mother.*

I sing your praises. You tell me,
I am Maya, goddess of illusion.
I am Grandmother, spinning past into future.

Your eight legs mirror your sectioned parts,
a balance between physical and spiritual.
You are weaver of magic who creates thread

from self and leaves to others to measure
and snip, destiny embodied in your very nature.
You, creator of spells, of language,

with designs meant to entice and confound —
you are not caught in your own creations
but glide over their spaces void with possibility.

I ask, *What do you want to tell me?* You reply, softly, *Be balanced and confident. Be assertive yet timid. Be who you are. Glide over doubts*

and space. Give birth and let your creation fend for itself. Weave comfort for your enemies then leave them in deep sleep. I listen with awe.

O Great Spider Mother, I plead, *will you return again and again in my dreams? I have more to learn, more to create, O Wise One.*

-for Ted Andrews

Sparrow

   Sparrow built its nest in easy access
to the outdoors on my Schmidt Family's farm,
in top spaces where door rollers needed to move.
Inside those dark chambers were scarecrow nests
of horse hair, string, straw, hay, dried weeds
that bulged out, hung down, forcing barn doors
to stay open. Sparrow would greet dawn with song
so my friend William was given earth-spirit-name,
"Golden Sparrow Singing to the Sunrise,"
a mantra for awakening of self in mornings
and throughout workday into lullaby of rest
for tomorrow's wonders. A symbiotic partner,
song and sun.
   Sparrow went about its business, whether sky
cloudy, dark, clear, rainy or bright, always quick
to escape pounce of predators, barn cats
and playful dog. A commoner among
cultured cardinal, oriole, goldfinch,
with drab brown streaked feathers, simple design,
only for dark spots on throat, a chakra for chirping.
   Sparrow was a survivor, hopping, searching,
pecking, bringing food back to young ones born
in cramped darkness. William is happy now,
rejoicing in tune to self or out loud, with sparrow,
his common partner, no needs, no worries.
   I observed my uncles only cleared the tracks
for frigid winters ahead to force these dark-earthed
itinerant squatters elsewhere. Sparrow obliged.

-for William Hurwitz

Traveling The Edge

Two late afternoons, I saw
      a red fox trotting in open field
          skirting woods on its way
somewhere. Houses all around.

      Civilization, its enemy. The first time,
          it was going; the next afternoon,
it was returning. I wondered where
      each time as if I were that lone creature

          endlessly going to and from,
not grasping sense of what journey
      was all about. Oh, yes, food,
          of course. I need it to nourish

self and those young ones
      back in the lair. Desires, too, that keep
          pulsating in and out, urging me
forward. Giving me purpose

      as if I sense their meaning.
          Like seasons of self that come
and go, fulfilled or waiting
      another turn at fulfillment.

          Like this trail, this primitive path
undestroyed by human progress.
      It projects its scent upward through
          macadam or gravel roadway.

Through grasses I jaunt. Even
       through houses, through living rooms, too.
            On journey, I carry head straight, tail
horizontal. Sometimes, bend nose to ground

       for scent of assurance. I become path
            I travel. Blend as one with edges
of environs I trot.
       I eat the joys I come upon. Bring rest

       back to my cave of hunger.
Distribute prey to young ones I nourish.
       Then regurgitate rest if needed.
            Camouflage self for more journeys.

Always, I travel this realm between worlds.
       Dusk and darkness. Dawn and full light.
       Between self-fulfilling
and self-fulfilled. Between murkiness

       and clairvoyance. A shifting into shapes
           others fail to recognize.
This concealment protects me.
       It offers me power to be who I am.

            Strong. Focused. Journeying
with confidence. Alone or with sole partner.
       Balanced in harmony in world I live.
            Always self-aware and self-assured.

Whether human or fox, I shape my essence
      to meet my needs. The female in me
           dominates even in my maleness.
I am one with my changing and in my changing,

      I am one with the power to achieve
           what I need to achieve.
Red fox energy attuned to my coming
      and going, my going and returning.

           Afternoons and mornings.
Dawn and dusk. Change shifting change.
      Fox and human, one inside the other.

ACKNOWLEDGMENTS

Gratitude is generously extended to these printers, editors, and/or publishers, for publication of the following poems:

"I Am Turtle," *Stoneboat.*
"Waters Turned Into Harp," *Deus Loci.* The International Lawrence Durrell Society.
"Dragonfly," *Third Wednesday.*
"Night Granary Rest," *Mad Poets Review.*
"Squirrel Self," *The Taylor Trust: Poetry & Prose.*
"A Bird's Lament," *Animals in Poetry.* SOULSPEAK/The Sarasota Theatre Press.
"Fair Warning," *Georgetown Review.*
"Visitor," *Oracle.*
"Gathering," *Willard & Maple.*
"Beach Walk," *Lake Effect.*
"Flesh Bait," *The Binnacle.*
"Mating Season," *Bellowing Ark.*
"Over Shimmering Water," *The Mid-America Poetry Review.*
"Return From Windham," *Plainsongs.* Also published in a different version as "From Windham" in *The Cape Rock.*
"The Prickly Ones," *The Pegasus Review.*
"On Meeting An Ant," *Kennesaw Review.* Published earlier as "On Meeting An Ant Midway Across The Floor."
"Tomorrow," *Tapestries, An Anthology.* LIFE Program, Mount Wachusett Com. College.

I also extend my appreciation to the Hudson Valley Writers' Center and poet Richard Blanco for their invaluable advice on putting this manuscript together. I'm also very grateful to Vermont Studio Center for my poetry residencies where some of these poems were written and others were fine tuned for ***MOVING TO COMPLETION***. Others have contributed their support, encouragement, and blessings: Louise von Weise and Jon Gregg; Kathy Black; Glennis Drew; Barbara Unger and Ted Sakano; Michael Burkard; Lois and Gary Joseph; Maryalice Johnston; Breahanna Schwartz; members of my Schmidt, Fitzpatrick, Gregorius, Wallace, Hubertus, Stapleton, Burgeson, Corry, Rodrigues, Beaton, Danielson Family; Bobbi Levin; Peter Occhiogrosso; Kathy Kiewel and Elliot Hurwitz and families; Fahim and Seema Mojawalla, novelist daughter Hibbah Mojawalla, other family members; Sam Sussman; Lee Squires and Michael Sussman, and all family members; Gloria and Macey Levin; Joanne Weber; Catherine Nolan; Ashok and Dina Dubey; Holly Reed and Jan Marks; Neil and Carmen Smoke, son Skyler; Heitzi Epstein and Geoffrey Green; Bruce and Nancy Green; Joan and Peter Schmidt, sons, and family; Sydney Babush; Leslie and Peter Walker; Peggy Walpole; Janet Schmidt; Owens, Milora, Tourneux families; Evelyn and Harry Babush; Jody R. LaGreca; Marilyn Maxwell and Pat Precin; Claire and Ed McCann; Sharon Stahl; Marion Stevens; Bonnie McCandless; Sandra Cohen; Isabel and Ludwig Glomb; Faith Palmer; Arthur Tuttle; Diane Hires; and Corrine Smith.

About Shelley Meisler:

Shelley Meisler has been creating and selling jewelry much of her life. She is a wild-life painter and avid gardener. In poetry, she has found a way to combine colorful imagery of painting and the delicate sculpturing of silver. She lives surrounded by woods and wonder in Warwick, NY. Her painting of red foxes is found with "**Traveling The Edge**."

About Todd Vogel:

Todd Vogel is a professional photographer, whose work is found throughout ***MOVING TO COMPLETION.*** He is a novelist, writer and publisher of small books on topics meant to help others deal with issues of self and life available on his web site, **ODATBooks.com.** He says of his work, "Todd Vogel is in awe of the natural world. This sense of wonder is what he tries to pass on in his images."

About Rob Stolzer

Rob Stolzer's work has appeared in *The New York Times Book Review*, *The Progressive*, and *The Chronicle of Higher Education*. For the last number of years, Stolzer has focused on his painting, which can be seen at www.robstolzer.com. Stolzer has taught in the Department of Art and Design at the University of Wisconsin-Stevens Point, since 1991. He is currently the Chair of the Department. His art work appears with "**I Am Turtle.**"

About Donald Revell:

Donald Revell is a poet/translator, teaching and living in Nevada. His most recent collection is *The Bitter Withy* (Alice James Books, 2009).

About The Poet:

John Fitzpatrick grew up roaming the woods on his maternal Schmidt grandparents' farm outside Dansville, NY, home of Clara Barton and her first American Red Cross Chapter. Now in Rhinebeck, he talks to trees, plants, stones and listens carefully to what they say. Animal-spirits have communicated with him also as evident by these poems in *Moving To Completion*. His poems have garnered honors and are widely published in American Literary magazines, as in *Untamed Ink*, *California Quarterly*, *Stone Voices*, *Chronogram*, *Out of Line*, *SLAB*, *City Works*, and *BIG MUDDY*. He has a poem on a CD, *Tree Magic: Nature's Antennas,* edited by Jackie Hofer, and in two books, *Belief Persists*, edited by Adrianna Delgado, and in *Collecting Life: Poets on Objects Known and Imagined*, edited by Madelyn Garner and Andrea L. Watson. He received the Hackney National Poetry Literary Award from Birmingham-Southern College and Vermont Studio Center poetry residencies. Fitzpatrick holds a BA from the University of Notre Dame, MS from Hofstra University, and Ph. D. from New York University with a dissertation that treated the poet as writer and reader of poetry, with poets Barbara Unger and Michael Burkard participating in his research. He taught English and founded and coached an award winning Speech-Debate Team at George W. Hewlett High, Long Island, for thirty years, and received the yearbook *Patches* dedication, the Hewlett-Woodmere School District's

Distinguished Service Award, and election to the Hewlett High Teacher Hall of Fame. From Notre Dame through its Alumni Association, he received its Excellence in Teaching Award. Fitzpatrick is also a certified Reconnective Healing Practitioner TM, a Usui Reiki Practitioner, and a Teacher of Kundalini Yoga as taught by Yogi Bhajan. *Moving To Completion* is John Fitzpatrick's first book of poetry. His blog is: http://turtleami.blogspot.com. His web page is: http://turtleami.com.

About This Book:

Moving To Completion reflects a fascination with nature and a communication with the spirit world found in myriad ways through sentient and insentient beings around us. Through poetry, photography, and art work, individual items of a turtle, sea shell, bird, fox, groups of sea life or migrating geese, all provide the reader with reflections that illustrate a personal perspective within universal possibilities. *Moving To Completion* motivates us to see simple ordinary animals in their own unique way. It shows a communication between nature's spirit and the creative human spirit which presents an energy of oneness. Through whatever artistic medium used, the poet/artist/photographer demonstrates a vision drawn that is at peace with the environment and the internal self, a common energy force within every element of the universe.